H

Coos

Granny and Grandad
aka Rosemary & Golin Girasoli

Nonna

Published in 2023 by Nonna Sunflower

ISBN Paperback: 978-1-7393676-0-2
Ebook: 978-1-7393676-1-9

A CIP catalogue copy of this book can be found in the British Library.

Published with the help of Indie Authors World
www.indieauthorsworld.com

Dedication:
Written for
Leo and Jesse Girasoli

Many years ago, there lived two Heilan' coos called Morag and Jimmy. Morag was a very pretty Heilan' coo, with long, curly, red hair. Her hair was always shaggy and knotted because of all the mischief she found herself in. Jimmy's hair was a lot more sophisticated, his long, red hair was straight and well-groomed. Afterall, Jimmy was always the more organised of the two!

Morag and Jimmy roamed freely in the Highlands of Scotland, spending their days walking through the mountains and over the fields, wandering around wherever and whenever they wanted. Morag and Jimmy ate the lush green grass, drank from the clear blue rivers, and played games together with nothing to worry them.

Morag and Jimmy were happy, but they often wondered if they were the only two Heilan' coos left in the whole wide world. As they roamed around the countryside, they never ever saw another coo that looked like them.

Jimmy did most of the work because Morag was a wee bit lazy. Morag liked to just lie down in the field or on the hills, soaking up the rain and the sunshine which made the grass a beautiful shade of green.

One day Jimmy said to Morag, "You have to help out and do some of the work!" So, reluctantly, Morag said that she would help Jimmy out.

Her first job was to take the plates and bowls down to the river to wash them.

Morag put all of the dishes on top of a small raft in the river so that she had something to lean on. However, as usual, Morag was not concentrating on the job she was doing! She was too busy looking at the clouds, watching all of the birds flying around, paddling about in the river and just dreaming her day away.

The next thing Morag knew, all of the plates had sailed down the river on the wee raft!

"Not again!" Morag shouted. Water went flying everywhere as she splashed around in the river to chase after the raft. *But, oh dear, Morag was too lazy* and too slow and, before she could catch them, they were gone, completely washed away by the river. Jimmy heard all of the commotion and ran down to help, but he was too late, Morag had lost all of the plates.

Jimmy was not a happy chappy, oh no he was not! He told Morag, "You must concentrate and pay attention when you are helping out."

"Ok," said Morag, but she really wasn't worried about it, they still had the bowls.

Och, Jimmy felt sorry for Morag, she looked so sad standing alone in the river. Her curly red hair was sopping wet and her fringe covered her eyes.

Morag managed to pull herself up onto the bank. But, oh no, unfortunately the silly coo was on the wrong side of the river! She couldn't get back over to the field that Jimmy was in.

Morag looked around in a panic. Maybe there was a bridge nearby that she could use? But, there was no bridge in sight. What was she going to do, how can she get back across the river? She can't swim!

Jimmy shouted across the river, "You're a big heavy animal, with a huge body, huge head and huge horns, there is a tree behind you, push it down, then roll it to the river and make a bridge."

Morag pushed and pushed but the tree wouldn't budge. She asked Jimmy to come and help her push because two big heavy coos would be much better than one and Jimmy was much bigger than her.

Jimmy crossed the river to help her. "WAIT A MINUTE, MORAG!" shouted Jimmy. "I've just walked across the river, it's only up to my elbows, you don't need a bridge, just walk across and climb out at the bank and you will be back in our field."

Morag felt very silly, she does tend to panic right away instead of taking time to think. They both crossed the river and got back to their own field. The panic was over and Jimmy was able to retrieve the wee raft...without the plates.

*

The next day Morag decided to really concentrate when she was washing the bowls, she didn't want to lose them. So, she placed the bowls on the wee raft and then she jumped on herself.

Was that a good idea? A big fat Heilan' coo sitting on a wee teeny-weeny raft?

I don't think so.

Morag was happily leaning over into the water, washing the bowls and placing them back on the raft, when the raft started to move, faster and faster and faster. Morag was so deep in concentration that she hadn't noticed until it was too late and, just as she heard the noise of the waterfall, the wee raft went over – with Morag still on it!

Morag clung onto the raft, thinking about where the raft could possibly end up now. She could sail all the way to the River Clyde in Glasgow, which was massive! How would she get back to the Highlands? She might never get to see Jimmy again, she should have listened to him and paid attention. Morag was so worried about getting lost she didn't even notice when some of the bowls fell off the raft and into the river!

But luckily the raft washed up on a small sandy bank not far from their field. Morag gathered up the remaining two bowls and calmly walked back to the field.

"Everything alright?" asked Jimmy.

"Wonderful," said Morag, as she put the bowls down.

She hoped he wouldn't notice that she had lost the raft and they were now down to two bowls!

*

Och, Morag was bored. She had recovered from her fright on the runaway raft a couple of days ago, and was just bored now of always walking around the same fields and hills all day long.

"I think it's time for an adventure," Morag said to herself.

So, she ventured a wee bit further up the hill all the way to a fence. It was the first fence she had ever seen and there was a huge building in the next field.

Morag wondered what was in the huge building. She would go get Jimmy and ask if he knew what it was, maybe they could have a look inside together?

Morag turned on her tail and started heading down the hill again to get Jimmy. As she was strolling down the hill and enjoying the scenery, she saw something big up ahead going across her path. Morag stopped. What was that? Suddenly two more of the same things ran across the path. They were big, black and bushy, running on four legs.

Morag ran all the way down to get Jimmy. Morag didn't want to admit it, but she was really scared to go on her own back up to the fence.

Luckily, Jimmy said he would go with her, but they would wait until it was really, really, really dark, probably when they could see the moon. "We don't want to get into trouble," said Jimmy.

As soon as it was dark Morag and Jimmy started walking up the hill. It was very dark with only the moon lighting their way, so they had to walk slowly. Even though they were walking slowly, they still managed to bump into and trip over the things around them. Morag brushed up against a very leafy tree branch and screeched. She jumped behind Jimmy, hiding away from whatever had touched her.

Jimmy hadn't seen the lazy coo move so fast before. "It's only a few leaves, you big baby," he laughed at her.

Morag humphed and they carried on. That's when they heard some shuffling and leaves rustling in the corner. Was that a shadow running through the trees? Two shadows? Three shadows?! And were those three pairs of eyes looking out at them from between the dark trees?

Jimmy stopped. "What's that?" he asked nervously.

Morag stopped beside him. "I didn't see anything," she said, refusing to look in the direction Jimmy was.

The trees rustled ahead of them and the eyes moved closer.

"Did you see that?" Jimmy asked again. "Are those eyes shining in the trees? Are they coming towards us?!"

"Just your fat feet making loads of noise!" Morag said back. Morag didn't want to admit that she'd seen the shadows and eyes, too, especially because she was huffing with him. She was still scared from seeing those hairy things in the woods earlier. "Come on, we have to find out what's in this big building," she said, not wanting to hang around.

They continued walking up the hill again, a little bit quicker this time. Neither of them wanted to admit that they felt like the eyes were following them, but they were too scared to look around and see.

They both felt better when they finally reached the fence and let out a sigh of relief.

Jimmy explained that it was a fence, and he remembered that they had had fences that kept them in when they were young calves. They couldn't get past the fence, they couldn't see a gate.

Morag said, "Jimmy, you are much bigger than me, break the fence down."

Jimmy was angry with Morag – fences must be erected for a reason. Maybe it was to keep the animals safe in a field, or to keep something out, like whoever owned those eyes earlier! You can't just break them down.

Luckily, they were both tall enough to simply step over the fence and walk into the next field.

They heard loud music coming from the building. Jimmy said the building was called a barn, he remembered that, many years ago when they were part of a large herd of Heilan' coos, they also had a barn. The music was getting louder and louder, maybe someone was holding a barn dance?

They both crept up to the barn and peeped through the gap in the wood. They could see a whole herd of Heilan' coos having a great old time singing and dancing. Jimmy and Morag really wanted to go to the barn dance, but, most importantly, they were delighted to see other coos that looked just like them for the first time since they were wee calves!

Just like that, the big barn doors flew open and out walked two very large coos.

"What are you doing here?" said the lady coo.

"Were you invited?" asked the big male coo in a very deep, gruff voice.

Oh dear, what excuse will Morag and Jimmy give? They shouldn't be in this field and they shouldn't be at the barn! They were both a wee bit worried, until the big male coo

started laughing at Morag and Jimmy's worried faces and they realised that the coos were only joking.

"Hiya, I'm Rab," said the big male coo.

"I'm Isa," said the lady coo. "Do you want to come into our barn dance?"

Well, you couldn't hold Morag and Jimmy back, they just ran straight into the barn and had a great old time.

Morag and Jimmy danced all night with the other Heilan' coos. Isa and Rab introduced them to lots of their friends, it turns out that they only lived a couple of fields over! One of Isa and Rab's friends was telling them about the lovely plates that washed up in the riverbank beside their field, and only the next day matching bowls appeared. The Heilan' coo loved her discovery. Morag pretended not to notice Jimmy looking at her as he thought about his own missing plates and bowls! Morag and Jimmy said they enjoyed themselves so much they would come again tomorrow night!

*

The very next day Morag and Jimmy were in their own field blethering away about the barn dance and how excited they were about another dance tonight, when a bird landed on Morag's nose.

Morag jumped about, twitched her ears and swished her tail trying to get it off. Jimmy told her, "Stand still and leave the wee bird alone, it will fly away soon."

However, Morag was worried. "What if the bird does a wee jobby and it fills my nostrils, I won't be able to breathe!" she said.

She really did have an overactive imagination.

"Och, don't be so silly," said Jimmy, "you can breathe through your mouth and, anyway, the bird is just eating the bugs on your fur."

WHAT?! WHAT BUGS?!

"I've got bugs, I've actually got bugs!"

Oh my goodness me, Morag was getting herself into a terrible state.

"Morag, Morag, calm down, Morag," said Jimmy.

Morag flopped to the ground flat as a pancake! Oh no, she's fainted and landed right on top of a large poo!

Jimmy rubbed her legs, while trying to avoid the poo, and he patted her face until she came around.

"What happened?" asked Morag.

"You were being a drama queen because a bird landed on your nose and you fainted," said Jimmy. "Come on now, Morag, we need to get ready for the barn dance tonight."

"My hair is a mess now, it looks like a burst couch! I can't go to the dance like this!" Morag cried.

Jimmy suggested that Morag should stand at the top of the hill where there was a gale blowing. This would sort out Morag's hair problem and maybe blow away the smell of poo as well!

Morag agreed with Jimmy and climbed up to the top of the hill. She turned this way and that, letting the winds fluff up her beautiful curly hair.

Once Morag was happy with her hair, and Jimmy had checked that the poo smell was away, they headed off to the next field.

Mmm, that's strange, I can't hear the music coming from the barn, Morag and Jimmy thought. *Och, we'll head up anyway, maybe Rab and Isa are having a wee rest.* Morag and Jimmy trotted over to the barn.

Just as they reached the barn door, it burst wide open! Oh no, there was Farmer Broon standing in the doorway, with a shotgun! Well, Morag and Jimmy didn't expect this.

The farmer shouted at them, "Get out of my field!" and raised his shotgun.

"RUN!" shouted Jimmy.

Morag and Jimmy turned on their tails and ran and ran until they were back in their own field – their home. They were both a wee bit scared, so they promised to stay in their safe field for a while until they felt safe again. They weren't going back to the barn anytime soon. They were more scared than they were the night they saw the shadows in the hills!

However, the very next morning Rab was standing at the fence waiting for them. "What happened to you two last night, why didn't you come to the barn dance?"

Morag nearly fainted again just thinking about last night, and she listened as Jimmy explained to Rab exactly what had happened.

"Och, you are a silly pair of coos, that's Farmer Hamish Broon! He's the one that feeds us and organises the barn, you must have given him a terrible fright," said Rab.

"WE gave HIM a fright, are you joking, he had a shotgun?!" shouted Jimmy.

Rab explained that Hamish was getting old and he thinks that there are still big bad wolves out in the hills just waiting to eat the coos. So, he carries the gun to protect his coos, but he has no bullets, and his coos don't want to upset him by telling him that there are no wolves in Scotland anymore.

There used to be wolves in Scotland? Morag thought. *Oh no, were they the creatures I saw, and the shadows from the other night? No, no, I'm sure that wasn't it, after all Rab says there are no more wolves in Scotland!*

Rab said that they should come to the barn dance tonight and he would introduce them to Hamish, so that he didn't make that mistake again. Jimmy and Morag happily agreed – they would love to go to the barn again, as they had such a great time last time.

*

That night Rab introduced Jimmy and Morag to Farmer Hamish and he welcomed them to his barn. He asked very strange questions like, "Who owns you? Where is the rest of your herd?" Farmer Hamish was very interested when they told him that they had been roaming the mountains and countryside of Scotland for many years and thought they were all alone in the world until they found his herd and their barn dance. Morag and Jimmy thought Farmer Hamish was the nicest man they had ever met.

They all joined Farmer Hamish outside as he watched for any potential wolves who would harm his Heilan' coos. Farmer Hamish was adamant that he had seen wolves in these woods before with his very own eyes.

Morag and Jimmy looked at each other worriedly. Rab had said there are no wolves in bonnie Scotland now, but could there be?

Morag and Jimmy told Farmer Hamish and Rab a wee story all about the strange things they had seen in the woods the other day. Morag told them about seeing the big, black, bushy creatures running across her path, and Jimmy told them about how they both saw three pairs of eyes watching them in the woods as well. Morag and Jimmy were becoming very certain that what they had been seeing was wolves in the woods nearby.

"Don't be silly, there are no wolves in Scotland anymore," Rab laughed at them.

Farmer Hamish didn't look so sure.

*

The very next day Morag and Jimmy were having a stroll around their hills and their woods. It was a bright day and they were enjoying feeling the sunshine soaking into their hair.

Wait, what was that up ahead?

It's the wolves running around in the woods!

Morag and Jimmy didn't know what to do. Should they run away again? What will they do?

Wait a minute, they heard voices. Morag and Jimmy hid behind two large trees just as two wee boys approached. Morag and Jimmy were very worried that the boys were running and playing in the woods when there were wolves around.

The two wee boys said, "Hello!" to Morag and Jimmy, and the coos nearly jumped out of their hair they got such a fright. "My name is Leo and this is my brother Jesse."

The coos gave their names and Jimmy said, "You have to run and hide boys, there are wolves in these woods!"

"Don't be silly, there are no wolves in Scotland now. You might be thinking of our dogs, their names are Lupo, Luna and Echo, although from a distance they do look a wee bit like wolves. Would you like to meet them? I promise they're not wolves."

Morag and Jimmy didn't believe them, but they agreed to meet their dogs. Leo and Jesse called over their pets, and the Heilan' coos were so happy to see that the animals that bounded over with their tails wagging were indeed dogs, although they really did look like wolves.

Morag and Jimmy asked the two wee boys to let Farmer Hamish see their 'wolves' so the old man wouldn't have to worry anymore about defending his herd. The wee boys happily agreed and they walked up to the barn with their three dogs and Morag and Jimmy. The group had a great time getting to know each other and playing with the three 'wolves'.

*

Somewhere in a lonely spot in the highlands of Scotland there are still wolves wandering around. At least, the authors hope so.

Morag and Jimmy are just glad it's nowhere near them!

About the Author

Rosemary is 72 years old and has been married to Colin for 48 years. They have two wonderful sons and two equally wonderful grandsons. Rosemary loves to travel and when she was younger hiked in various countries including the Andes and on the Inca Trail, in Bhutan in the Himalayas, the Alps in Europe, not forgetting the fabulous Cairngorms in Bonnie Scotland! She is looking forward to many more adventures. However, they will be at a quieter pace.

Ingram Content Group UK Ltd.
Milton Keynes UK
UKHW050618210623
423796UK00010B/63

9 781739 367602